SUPER ROOT SPICES

First published in the United Kingdom in 2019 by
Pavilion, 43 Great Ormond Street, London WC1N 3HZ

ISBN 978-1-91162-411-0

A CIP catalogue record for this book is available from
the British Library

10 9 8 7 6 5 4 3 2 1

Printed and bound by 1010 Printing International Ltd, China

www.pavilionbooks.com

Neither the author nor the publisher can accept
responsibility for any injury or illness that may arise as a
result of following the advice contained in this work. Any
application of the information contained in the book is at
the reader's sole discretion.

The oven temperatures listed within this book are for
conventional ovens. If using a fan oven, reduce the heat by
20°C. Be aware that oven temperatures may vary.

SUPER ROOT SPICES

Zoë Lind van't Hof
and Tom Smale

PAVILION

Clockwise from top-left:
burdock root, astragalus
root, fo-ti (he shou wu),
shatavari root, pau d'arco

The Story Behind Us

Our golden journey to Wunder Workshop

My late mother and I (Zoë) visited Sri Lanka twice during my teenage years and we fell in love with its magic, the warm people, the beautifully diverse landscape, the divine food and the wisdom within Ayurveda, its traditional medical system. We had learned about Ayurveda during our first visit when we had stayed at an Ayurvedic retreat. Each day I would sit with a qualified Ayurvedic doctor and we would discuss at length its traditions and approach to health. During this visit one spice stood out above all others and that was the vibrantly bright turmeric root. It was used in most of the dishes that we ate, and we drank a concoction made from milk, turmeric and black pepper after our yoga sessions. I even experienced turmeric facemasks and soaked my feet in turmeric water.

The healing plants and the ancient wisdom of Ayurveda fascinated me, so on my next visit I planned to travel deeper into Sri Lanka. On my travels in the Kandy Mountains, I met the owner of a turmeric farm and this is where my golden journey began. To follow an intuition or at least act upon an urge to evolve and challenge the status quo requires self-acceptance and self-respect. There is true magic in finding and listening to the voice within and acting upon instinct. I am fully aware that this might just sound like a lot of numinous hoo-ha, but I believe that when we busy ourselves with life we can become out of tune with our deepest aspirations.

During this trip to Sri Lanka, I thankfully dared to cultivate that inner voice and evolve my inner passion, a passion that had always been right there in front of me – health and food. A passion passed on to me by my mother, who truly embodied a holistic lifestyle for over 40 years through her work as a natural and holistic beauty therapist. Our house was always strewn with books about plant-based medicines, superfoods, Ayurveda, herbs and botanical concoctions. These books had drawn my curiosity from a young age.

Everything seemed to come together: my upbringing surrounded by health and wellbeing; discovering the most enlightening book, *The Power of Now: A Guide to Spiritual Enlightenment* by Eckhart Tolle; making a New Year's resolution to leave my job to follow my dreams; and returning to Sri Lanka. I didn't know it then, but the principles of Ayurveda embodied the transformation that was occurring. Ayurveda literally translates as the 'science of life' and this ancient healing system places significance on the mind, body and spirit. It believes that everyone has the responsibility for their own health by understanding their body and emotions, and by living life moment to moment – in exactly the way I hadn't done up until this point.

Often we do not credit ourselves for the steps we take, albeit small ones, on our constantly evolving path. When I look back at the time I made my decision to jump into the uncertainty and insecurity of running my own company, I feel immensely grateful for the courage that was residing within me and also for the loving support from my mother who accompanied me without judgement on my new path. Maybe my decision was sprinkled with a tinge of naivety, a characteristic so close to vulnerability. But at that time I remember feeling the strong need to nurture my soul. It felt like the perfect time to meander into the unknown.

Embarking on my path to start a turmeric business didn't start as smoothly as I had imagined. It was scattered with obstacles right from the beginning. Two days before my last day at work, my flat was burgled while I was asleep. I awoke to find that everything I deemed valuable was gone: my laptop, my wallet, my designer bag, jewellery, sunglasses, watch and many more 'things'. My notebooks containing thoughts and business ideas were gone too – carefully written down plans were now just thoughts in my mind. People commented that I should see it as a 'sign' and continue working in a safe job that would pay my bills and allow me to buy back these 'things'. On reflection, ironically I treasure this experience as I learned that these were only material losses. The experience, in fact, affirmed my beliefs and made me realize that my motivation to start a business was not driven by the desire to make lots of money. Instead, I found value in doing what I loved, spending time with my family and friends. This proved to bring me more happiness than any material belonging ever could. Not least because another major event in my life was just around the corner, one that would emphasize this feeling even further.

Destiny can be a strange thing: it had never occurred to me that perhaps all the changes that I was making to improve my own life actually held a much higher purpose. The timing could not have been more significant either, as at no other time in my life did I feel so confident and grounded, and yet I was to be truly uprooted by the news that one month into starting my business my mother was diagnosed with metastatic breast cancer.

No one could believe it. My mother, who was radiant with life and youthfulness, had cancer. She was the most active and resilient woman I have ever met, so the idea that she would become weak and powerless was a very big shift. This pivotal event put my whole life into perspective. It made me realize that my decision to start my own business was the right decision, as it gave me the flexibility that no other job could ever have done at that time. Together with my aunt we cared for my mother from home. What struck me was that all the knowledge, love and gratitude she had taught me throughout my life, I now had to give to her. We saw the cancer as a temporary inconvenience and she outlived all of the doctors' predictions, but passed away just over a year after her diagnosis.

Learning to live with grief has been a whole new lesson. Life can be so clear and yet so dark at the same time, but it is in realizing that these things go hand in hand, like yin and yang, that you become aware that you cannot feel the beauty without the beast. Experiencing my mother in the wake of her illness was as if someone had put a magnifying glass on the love that we had to give each other. Towards the end of her life I began to realize that a beautiful circle was closing.

Since that time, my boyfriend and now business partner, Tom, has supported me through the tough years, leaving his own job in finance to jump into the uncertainty and embrace the unknown.

Tom has always been fascinated by health and the workings of the body. A love of sport from a young age, particularly rugby, grew into an interest in nutrition and how best to sustain energy levels, fitness and aid recovery afterwards. At university in Manchester, through Tom's studies in pharmacology, it became clear to him that inflammation was an instrumental part of many disease processes and limiting inflammation was, and still is, an important part of disease regulation and prevention. Which is one of the reasons why turmeric and its anti-inflammatory qualities, among many other properties, sparked Tom's interest. It became clear that curcumin, the active ingredient in turmeric, along with other compounds in the spice root were beneficial for treating a variety of illnesses and turmeric's effect on inflammation was a natural way to limit damage in the body when in a diseased state. While much of the research at that time focused on isolated compounds, due to the safeguarding and patenting mentality of those funding research, the use of turmeric as a whole could clearly be helpful, too, if consumed in the right way and combined with certain other ingredients to improve absorption.

Tom's solid understanding of pharmacokinetics and bioavailability has been important to Wunder Workshop's own product development. Every product we create is designed to maximize the bioavailability of the ingredients used.

With this in mind we have made Wunder Workshop what it is today. A brand created out of passion for traditional medicine, from the nurturing love and knowledge from my mother that inspired me, and the dedication that we both have in creating more awareness about miraculous turmeric (and other healthy roots and ingredients) that we believe nurture and support our health.

About this Book

This book was inspired by our passion for using nature's most nutritious ingredients. We're on a mission at Wunder Workshop to create delicious ways for people to incorporate turmeric and other wonder roots and spices into their lives with innovative food, drink and beauty products. In this book, we share many of these recipes as well as those we enjoy making at home and on our travels, with the aim of bringing more vibrancy and purpose to the ingredients we eat, drink and use on our skin.

These recipes include a wider range of nutritious super roots and spices than simply turmeric and are inspired by our research over the years as well as by our travels to Sri Lanka and beyond, and our interest in traditional medical systems from the Far East to South America.

Many of these recipes combine ancient wisdom with modern techniques. We are particularly interested in using roots with medicinal qualities, or, as we like to call them, 'super roots'. They are not just used for their flavour, but to nurture and support the body and mind as well. We believe in 'eating with a purpose' and that every meal is an opportunity to nourish ourselves. So while the recipes taste great, we have created them to be functional, too, by maximizing the bioavailability of the ingredients and making super root spices more accessible.

Let food be thy medicine and medicine be thy food.

Hippocrates, father of medicine, 431 BCE

We see our recipes as an invitation to be creative with medicinal root spices and as a way of introducing them to your daily routine. All the roots we use have been celebrated in traditional medicine for their healing properties and have been used for thousands of years by indigenous people, but we urge you to do your own research and let your intuition guide you on what is right for you and your body. Using healing root spices should be part of a balanced diet and lifestyle. Most of our recipes are plant based, which is a representation of how we like to eat, but feel free to use them as inspiration and add fish, meat or dairy as you wish.

Zoë and Tom's Journey – Back to our Roots

Many of the recipes in this book have been inspired by our travels along with our family backgrounds and passion for roots. Sri Lanka and India, Primorsky Krai in southeast Russia, China, and the Brazilian Amazon all have particular importance for us. That said, we've also included root spices traditionally found in Europe and North and South America.

Sri Lanka & India

As with every new country I travel to, even in Europe, the first thing I do is visit a local food store to check out what is different. In Sri Lanka this is the most delightful experience, walking into tiny, dusty shops to find sacks of interesting looking twigs, roots and dried spices or pots with beautiful labels. Fortunately, I have often been accompanied on my trips to shops, magical spice gardens and markets by an Ayurvedic doctor, who takes time to explain the different roots and spices and their use in treatments and meals. The welcoming hospitality of the Sri Lankans has led me to visit many homes where the moment I mention my interest in traditional roots and spices, I am treated to all kinds of exciting concoctions and tinctures – as well as the usual tea and biscuits.

Roots and spices play a fundamental part of Ayurveda, the traditional medical system of India and Sri Lanka. It has been practised for at least 5,000 years and is still one of the most sophisticated holistic health systems, focusing on treating both body and mind. There are so many beneficial roots used in Ayurvedic medicine, too many to mention in great detail, hence why we have selected a few or our favourites for this book: turmeric, ashwagandha, liquorice, shatavari and ginger.

Primorsky Krai, Far East Russia

During travels to explore my family heritage in Far East Russia, I stumbled across adaptogen herbs (an adaptogen is a herb that improves the body's natural ability to deal with stress), both in a small market in Ussuriysk and on a foraging trip in the beautiful countryside of this part of Russia. I was aware of the adaptogens, ginseng and rhodiola, but I didn't realize that they originated from this part of Russia.

It was fascinating to discover that this region where my grandmother grew up is a real storehouse of medicinal plants. Unsurprisingly, the herbs and spices that grow in this region have adapted to survive all weather extremes, which span dramatically throughout the seasons from arctic to subtropical. Historically, the people of this region have often relied on these plants to strengthen their immune system to be able to survive the harsh weather conditions and this has influenced our choice of roots to focus on in this book. The following have been collected since ancient times in this region: panax ginseng, Siberian ginseng (eleuthero), rhodiola (also called golden root) and dandelion.

The Amazon

The indigenous people of the Amazon basin have a rich history of using plants for medicinal purposes. With Tom's heritage reaching back to indigenous tribes in Brazil through his grandmother, we were both keen to delve deeper into the richness of the roots from this region. More recently, Tom's familial connection to the 'lungs of the World', has been through his aunt, a research biologist at Kew Gardens, who has spent many years researching plants in the Amazon and even discovered a new plant species there, the *Licania sothersae*.

Roots are used in many ways in this part of the world, especially as the richness of the rainforest provides the perfect source for new and unique plants. Of course, many of these are yet to be studied for their medicinal benefits by western medical standards, but they have been used for generations to treat the maladies of the local people.

With so many different types of roots that grow in this vast and diverse landscape, it was difficult to choose only a few to mention in this book. Many non-indigenous plants now grow there such as turmeric, which is grown as a cheaper alternative to saffron and explains its name *açafrão da terra* (saffron of the ground). Our selection is based on those that are now readily available in the West, ranging from adaptogens and recognized superfoods to celebrated aphrodisiacs: suma (Brazilian ginseng), maca and muira puama.

Roots – the essential, fundamental, or primary part or nature of something.

China

Traditional Chinese Medicine (TCM) has evolved over at least 5,000 years and takes a holistic approach to disease. Similar to Ayurveda, it focuses as much on the prevention of disease as on treating it. Many thousands of years ago, TCM was divided into four different areas, of which dietary physicians were awarded the highest status compared to the other three: internal medicine, external medicine and veterinary medicine. Diet still plays an integral part in TCM.

The Chinese use thousands of different spices, barks, minerals, flowers, mushrooms and roots in their medicines, yet we have had to be select in our choice and focus on the super roots astragalus, burdock, ginger, panax ginseng, fo-ti (he shou wu), liquorice and rhodiola.

Why Super Roots?

Often the answer lies in the meaning of the word... the dictionary defines roots as 'part of the body of a plant that grows downward into the soil, anchoring the plant and absorbing nutriment and moisture'. The term, root, is also commonly used to describe 'the essential, fundamental, or primary part or nature of something'. The latter is at the heart of our philosophy. Essential nutrients are concentrated in the root and they are the lifeline of a plant, with its ability to draw in water and minerals from the ground. This means that when harvested, roots can contain nutrients that are not found in other parts of the plant.

Many of the super roots in this book have specific therapeutic properties, including:

Adaptogenic: can improve our natural ability to deal with stress and restore balance to body and mind. Super roots that qualify as adaptogens include: panax ginseng, ashwagandha, astragalus, Siberian ginseng, fo-ti, liquorice, rhodiola, maca, muira puama and shatavari.

Nootropic: used to improve cognitive functioning and are also known as 'smart drugs'. The name comes from the Greek 'noos' for 'mind'. Super roots with nootropic qualities include: rhodiola, liquorice and ashwagandha.

Nervine: benefit and support the nervous system. Super roots that qualify include: ashwagandha, Siberian ginseng and rhodiola.

Tonic herbs: also known as superior herbs, used to tone and invigorate certain systems in the body and increase and strengthen physiological energy. This includes the super roots ashwagandha, turmeric, Siberian ginseng, liquorice, ginger and fo-ti.

Quality

Quality is key. The healing power of root spices can only be as good as the quality of the raw ingredients. Choose organic roots (and other ingredients) whenever possible. They may be slightly more expensive, but quality costs more and since many of the recipes in this book require cooking and soaking the roots, you don't want to create a pesticide soup.

Buying organic root spices also means you are avoiding genetically modified ingredients (GMOs), artificial colourings, heavy metals and fillers. Non-organic turmeric, in particular, is often bulked out with fillers such as cornflour, chalk or sawdust and yellow colouring. For us, as a fully organic brand, we use third-party tests in order to make sure we only supply the highest quality turmeric.

Non-organic spices are often irradiated, which is used to reduce bacteria but also changes the chemical composition of the spice, diminishing the natural enzymes and vitamin levels.

How to Store

Mycotoxins (mould toxins) can be found in both herbs and spices; therefore, to avoid spoilage, it's important to store them in a glass jar or airtight container, rather than a paper box. The latter is prone to attracting moisture from the air and cooking, and the contents subsequently become a breeding ground for mould growth. Spices should never be kept for longer than a couple of months, so just buy what you need and don't let them go to waste in the back of the kitchen cupboard.

Fresh roots are best used soon after buying and should be stored in the refrigerator. The root should be firm and not wrinkly, without any discoloration. Once a fresh root becomes bendy, then it is usually past its best.

Bioavailability

Many foods work synergistically, meaning that they need the help of another ingredient before their nutrients can be fully absorbed and used by the body. The absorption of nutrients (or bioavailability) is also influenced by how an ingredient is cooked, prepared and how well it is digested. For us, it's vital that our super root products and recipes are as bioavailable as possible – it ties in with our belief that food is medicine.

A good example of where combining foods yields rewards is with the active compound curcumin in turmeric, which on its own has a low bioavailability. The reason for this is that curcumin is a relatively large molecule and struggles to pass through the gut wall lining of the intestine into the bloodstream, where it can deliver its anti-inflammatory and antioxidant benefits. Scientists have discovered that this can be altered by combining turmeric with black pepper, which contains a molecule called piperine that is able to bind with the curcumin and draw it into the bloodstream without negatively affecting its properties.

High-fibre foods, coffee, raw honey and healthy fats such as coconut, olive or rapeseed oil also have the ability to enhance the absorption of the nutrients found in super roots.

Similarly, the method of preparation is influential. For instance, extracting nutrients from herbal blends in the form of tea, by decocting it over time in hot water, creates a condensed solution of phytonutrients that are readily absorbed by the body. Also, don't forget fermentation, a fascinating chemical process that creates many additional nutritional benefits in a food, benefitting the gut flora.

Our Favourite Super Roots

Turmeric

Turmeric is perhaps one of the world's most divine and powerful roots. Its bright orange, golden colour and range of health benefits have captured the West's attention in recent years. We name this spice a real miracle food, having such a variety of health benefits.

The turmeric root, *Curcuma longa*, is a member of the ginger family of Zingiberaceae. It thrives in the hot, wet climates of southern Asia, from where it originates and grows up to 1 metre (3 feet) tall. The plant itself branches extensively with leaves growing up to 50cm (20 inches) wide and flowers with beautiful inflorescences of white, yellow and blue.

Turmeric's benefits derive from the polyphenol curcumin, which is one of over 300 compounds found in the turmeric rhizome. Curcumin is turmeric's most potent active ingredient and responsible for its famously distinct orange colour, giving rise to its most ancient use as a dye for clothes. However, it is curcumin's range of effects on the human body that are most fascinating and consequently it has been used in traditional medicine for thousands of years.

Curcumin is pleiotropic, meaning that it affects multiple genes and biological pathways in the body. Its complex array of actions has been utilized by traditional medicine systems for centuries, and more recently has piqued the interest of the western scientific community. The diversity of curcumin's actions is remarkable but we only have room to give a few of the key health benefits. What we find the most fascinating is that turmeric is not limited to its use in cuisine and can be applied in many different forms to have different effects on the body. Curcumin's role in inflammation is key to understanding its many other beneficial actions.

Ashwagandha (Indian Ginseng)

Ashwagandha is an adaptogenic root, and charmingly means 'smell of horse' in Hindi, due to its horsey aroma. However, we have noticed once it is combined with other ingredients the smell disappears. Ayurvedic medicine in India and Sri Lanka uses the dried root widely, due to its numerous qualities. It is mainly used for its adaptogenic, antioxidant, immune-boosting, anti-inflammatory and nervine properties. It has a direct effect on the endocrine system, stimulating the thyroid and therefore being beneficial for hypothyroidism. It's nervine qualities, make it particularly useful for treating anxiety and stress-induced issues such as depression.

Astragalus

Astragalus is an adaptogenic root and was traditionally used for its mood-uplifting, antioxidant, antibacterial and immune-boosting properties, and as a cardiovascular tonic. It is native to China, and its Chinese name means 'yellow leader', as it is considered one of the leading tonic herbs. It's a warming spice root that has been recognized by western medicine for its immune-boosting qualities.

Burdock

Burdock's dark roots have been used in Traditional Chinese Medicine for many centuries, predominantly for treating and preventing infections, for blood sugar regulation, as a blood purifier and as a diuretic. Due to its antibacterial qualities it is prescribed for sore throats, the common cold and to help restore the proper function of the body. Interestingly, in Europe, it is also used for lowering blood sugar, as its inulin content (a prebiotic fibre) is particularly suitable to lower blood sugar and improve digestion.

Opposite, clockwise from top-left: horseradish, galangal, panax ginseng, galangal, panax ginseng

Galangal

Galangal root is part of the ginger rhizome family and has many similar benefits to turmeric. Traditionally used in Thailand and China, it is widely available through Southeast Asia and is particularly prevalent in Indonesia and known as a fundamental ingredient in the Indonesian Jamu turmeric tonic. Galangal's anti-inflammatory qualities, similar to those of turmeric, can have a positive impact on several diseases including arthritis, cancer, heart disease and Alzheimer's disease.

Ginger

Ginger is another fantastic anti-inflammatory root that has been used for centuries in Ayurvedic and Traditional Chinese Medicine. It's renowned for its powerful bioactive compound gingerol, which has many medicinal benefits, mainly known for its strong anti-inflammatory and antioxidant properties. Its stimulating yet soothing flavour also helps to relieve nausea and is great for reducing pain from menstrual cramping. Similar to turmeric, it has been shown to be as effective as ibuprofen. Alongside turmeric we use this flavoursome root in most of our daily recipes.

Ginseng (Asian Ginseng, Panax Ginseng)

Ginseng root is probably one of the most widely used super roots in both Asian and western countries. Especially in the Orient it was seen as a superior tonic herb, where it translates as 'man root' in Chinese. It is one of the most studied roots and its bioactive compounds ginsenosides are known for their inhibitory effect in chronic inflammation, for their adaptogen qualities, for being a central nervous system stimulant and for their ability to enhance depleted immune system function.

Horseradish

Horseradish root is a refreshing and stimulating root that is closely related to wasabi and mustard. Its stimulating effect can energize and help carry blood to all parts of the body, it can also control immune system activity and provide congestion relief. However, please note that due to its diuretic quality, it might exacerbate symptoms related to irritable bowel syndrome.

Fo-ti (He Shou Wu)

This antioxidant-rich root's name translates as 'black haired Mr', but, don't worry, it won't make you hairy, it was named after the person who discovered it. Fo-ti is native to China, Japan and northern Vietnam. In modern Chinese herbal medicine this tonifying root is used to treat the blood, kidneys and liver. Fo-ti can also be used for anaemia as it's a good source of iron. It's also used to fight premature greying, impotence and dizziness. The most common way to consume this root traditionally is steamed with black beans.

Liquorice

Liquorice is another interesting adaptogen root that is antiviral, an antioxidant, anti-inflammatory and acts as an immunomodulator. In China and the Middle East it has been used for centuries as a medicine and is considered one of the principal root spices. It is also a phytoestrogen and is therefore used to balance oestrogen hormone levels. As with many of the other roots covered in this book it has anti-inflammatory qualities, and combined with its hormone-balancing qualities it's a great root to remember for easing discomfort during menstruation.

Maca

Energy boosting Maca has a very warm vanilla and caramel aroma and is a great root to add to baking and tonics. Maca's use can be traced back 2,000 years to indigenous Peruvians. It grows under extreme weather conditions in the peaks of the Andes, and these severe growing conditions have created another hardy super root full of nutrients. It was treasured by the Incas and in the 1500s the Spanish explorers who saw its benefits whilst conquering Peru decided to bring it back to Spain where its use was first restricted only to Spain's royalty as a fertility and energy enhancer. To this day maca is renowned for increasing potency and stamina.

Rhodiola

Rhodiola rosea has important medical indications that have been used for thousands of years. Despite this, it is under pressure in many of its indigenous regions, such as Bulgaria, due to poor conservation. The 'golden root' is commonly found in some of the colder areas of the world, high in the Himalayas, in northern Russia, Scandinavia and the Alps. It is packed with beneficial rosavins, flavonoids, terpenes and essential oils that are attributed to its adaptogenic, performance-enhancing and antidepressant properties. It is also a nootropic and is used for improving our cognitive ability and mental endurance and lowering chances of burnout.

Shatavari

Shatavari is a member of the Asparagacae family, indigenous to the Indian subcontinent. Growing up to 2 metres (6½ feet) tall, shatavari has been referenced in a number of ancient Ayurvedic works for its ability to influence lactation, which is why it is referred to as 'having one hundred roots', cleverly adapted to 'having one hundred husbands', a clear indication to its ability to boost female reproductive capacity and health. This is because it contains natural phytoestrogens that help throughout the female reproductive system, whilst in men it is said to have aphrodisiac qualities.

Siberian Ginseng (Eleuthero)

Not to be confused with Asian Panax Ginseng, Siberian Ginseng has long been used in Traditional Chinese Medicine and its vitality boosting properties have been listed in records dating back to the 1500s. It is distinct from other ginsengs for its lack of ginsenosides, the active compounds found in panax ginseng. Despite this, it is recognized as an adaptogen, having demonstrated endurance-enhancing properties and the ability to regulate adrenal function. It has also shown immunomodulatory potential, increasing white blood cell activity and function, helping to strengthen the immune system.

Marshmallow Root

Althea officinalis the scientific name for marshmallow is interesting as the genus *althea* translates as 'to heal' in Greek. Modern day marshmallow production is a far cry from the traditional medical uses for the plant. However, it is still recognized as a healer for irritated mucous membranes, sore throats and ulcers. It has an ability to form a thin protective layer for inflamed skin, thus providing relief for minor wounds. It has also shown potential for asthma and bronchitis.

Marshmallow root history dates back to the ancient Egyptians, where its intake was limited to the privileged. Early preparations included boiling the root with honey and it was used to alleviate the same problems as today. Our use in this book sticks to more traditional preparations rather than the campfire variety.

Nettle Root

If, like me, the word nettle brings back memories of itchy legs and desperately searching for a dock leaf, then the idea of consuming this plant probably isn't very appealing. However, nettle has been used for many centuries as a medicine for water retention and urinary issues. It is often recommended for benign prostatic hyperplasia (enlarged prostate), to aid urination. It has a potent diuretic effect that is useful as a natural cleanser for urinary tract infections, kidney stones, ulcers in the digestive tract and even gout. However, because of this diuretic effect it must be taken with caution as it can cause low blood pressure and interact with blood thinning and other cardiovascular related medication.

Other uses not related to its diuretic effect take advantage of its anti-inflammatory and analgesic properties which are useful for joint pain.

Valerian Root

Valerian is a root recognized by the MHRA (Medicines and Healthcare products Regulatory Agency) in the UK as a medicinal herb. The root has been recorded in archives as far back as Hippocrates, who prescribed it for insomnia. It is now known to act on GABA receptors, the same location that pharmaceutical benzodiazepines target for their tranquilizing effect. It is very much a staple ingredient for alleviating insomnia, anxiety and nervous conditions.

Muira Puama

Also known as 'potency wood', muira puama, native to the Amazonian basin is a root that has been used by indigenous Indians for many years as a powerful aphrodisiac to cure impotency and increase libido in both men and women. It is also used as a general health tonic, for rheumatism, vitality and memory.

Suma (Brazilian Ginseng)

Suma (*Pfaffia paniculata*) has a wide range of applications as a functional food and is often referred to as 'para toda' translating as 'for everything'. The root is commonly found in the Amazonian basin and has a dense root system that extends deep into the ground.

Suma is recognized as an adaptogen, with the ability to improve the body's resistance to external stressors, like environment, physical and psychological stress. It's adaptogenic effect helps to balance hormonal responses in the body, maintaining homeostasis. It is also renowned as an aphrodisiac and is often used as a natural sexual stimulant. There are many beneficial saponins found in Suma, even a specific class labelled pfaffosides that are thought to have anti-cancer properties. Its diverse use in traditional medical preparations and various findings in more modern research mean that Suma is a root well worth incorporating into our diets.

Mylks

Iced Golden Mylk

Prep: 10 minutes
Serves: 5

This is the mylk recipe that kicked off our company, Wunder Workshop, and brings back many fond memories. It is both creamy and refreshing and although best served straight away, it will keep in the refrigerator for up to 3 days. We also like to make it with homemade oat milk (see page 30). To do so, simply leave out the coconut and replace the water with the same quantity of oat milk.

125g/4½oz/1¾ cups desiccated (shredded) coconut

1.5l/52fl oz/6½ cups water

100g/3½oz/½ cup dried soft pitted dates, roughly chopped

1 tsp turmeric powder or ½ tsp chopped fresh turmeric root

½ tsp vanilla extract

pinch of black pepper

pinch of Himalayan sea salt

ice cubes

Put all the ingredients, apart from the ice, in a high-speed blender and blend for 1 minute on the highest setting or until smooth and creamy.

Strain the mixture through a nut milk bag or sieve lined with muslin (cheesecloth). Give the bag or cloth an occasional squeeze to extract as much liquid as possible – you may want to wear plastic gloves when straining the mixture to avoid staining your hands with turmeric.

The mylk is best served chilled but be aware that if left in the refrigerator the oil from the coconut will separate so it will need a good stir before serving. Serve the mylk over ice.

Golden Beetroot Latte

Prep and cook: 10 minutes
Serves: 1

Beetroot is a good source of iron and folate (naturally occurring folic acid). It also contains nitrates, betaine, magnesium and numerous antioxidants, notably betacyanin. The nitrates help the body to produce nitric oxide, which is said to lower blood pressure, while natural sources of betaine are shown to have anti-inflammatory and antioxidant benefits.

1 small fresh raw beetroot (beet)

3cm/1¼in piece of fresh root ginger

¼ tsp cayenne pepper

240ml/8fl oz/1 cup oat milk, preferably homemade (see below)

1 tsp Golden Spoon Turmeric Honey (Wunder Workshop or see page 92)

Juice the beetroot and ginger. Pour the juice into a mug and stir in the cayenne pepper.

Gently heat the oat milk until it almost reaches the boil.

Gradually pour the hot oat milk into the mug, stirring. Stir in the turmeric honey until well combined.

Oat milk
To make oat milk, use 200g/7oz/1½ cups organic rolled oats (oatmeal) for each 1 litre/35fl oz/4¼ cups water. Add to a blender with a pinch of salt, a drop of vanilla extract and sweeten to taste. Blend until creamy then strain the mixture through a nut milk bag or sieve lined with muslin (cheesecloth). Store the milk in a glass bottle and keep in the refrigerator for up to 3 days.

31

Wunder Woman – Super-Root Power Mylk

Prep and cook: 10 minutes
Serves: 1

Shatavari in Sanskrit literally translates as 'a woman who has a hundred husbands', a suggestion of the root's effectiveness in supporting the female reproductive system. The root is highly regarded in Ayurvedic medicine and is used to treat women of all ages, although they are not the only ones to benefit, since the root is believed to support men's fertility too. Similarly, maca, the Peruvian super root, has long been used to enhance sexual health.

240ml/8fl oz/1 cup oat milk, preferably homemade (see page 30)

1 tbsp maca powder

1 tsp shatavari root powder

½ tsp rhodiola root powder

½ tsp yacon root powder (a great low GI sweetener)

1 tbsp coconut butter, such as Coconut Manna

pinch of organic edible dried rose petals, to decorate (optional)

Gently heat the milk in a small pan. Add the other ingredients, except for the rose petals, and heat until the milk almost reaches the boil, whisking continuously until frothy. (If you have a milk steamer, add all of the ingredients together and steam until hot and frothy.)

Pour into a mug and sprinkle rose petals over the top, if using. This recipe makes a soothing drink to unwind busy bodies, to help restore and prepare for rest or play.

Muscle Mylk

Prep and cook: 10 minutes
Serves: 1

This is our go-to mylk after workouts and any form of exercise. The hemp protein contains the full complement of amino acids that build muscle and aid recovery. The combination of spice roots helps to promote circulation and reduce inflammation, two attributes that are key to limiting delayed onset muscle soreness (DOMS), which your body can feel after a hard workout. Triphala, an Ayurvedic blend of three herbs (amla, haritaki and bibhitaki), is celebrated for its immune-boosting and detoxifying qualities, targeting muscles and circulation.

240ml/8fl oz/1 cup plant-based milk, such as almond or oat milk (see page 30)
1 tbsp hemp protein powder
½ tsp Siberian ginseng powder
½ tsp ground ginger
½ tsp burdock root powder
½ tsp triphala powder
sweetener to taste, preferably raw honey or date syrup (optional)

Gently heat the milk in a small pan. Stir in the other ingredients, except for the sweetener, and heat until the milk almost reaches the boil, whisking continuously until frothy. (If you have a milk steamer, add all the ingredients together and steam until hot and frothy.)

Pour into a mug and sweeten with raw honey or date syrup, if you like. If using honey, make sure to add it to the mug, rather than the boiling milk in the pan to preserve its health benefits.

Golden Glow

This blend is designed to make you glow from the inside out. The combination of hormone-balancing maca and stress-reducing Siberian ginseng will help to promote healthy skin. Rice bran solubles are high in vitamin E, while turmeric's anti-inflammatory and antioxidant benefits help the skin to radiate health. Brahmi is a brain-boosting nootropic herb believed to improve cognitive function. It is widely used in Ayurveda for mental agility and memory.

500ml/17fl oz/2 cups oat milk, preferably homemade (see page 30)
2 tbsp maca powder
1 tbsp turmeric powder
2 tsp Siberian ginseng powder
1 tsp brahmi powder
1½ tsp rice bran solubles (tocos)
pinch of black pepper

Gently heat the milk in a small pan.

Mix together all the powders with the rice bran solubles and black pepper in a bowl. Stir in a splash of hot water to make a thin paste.

Add the paste to the warm oat milk and stir well until combined. Heat until the milk almost reaches the boil, stirring. Pour into two mugs and serve.

Golden Night Cap

Prep and cook: 10 minutes
Serves: 1

Valerian root has long been recognized as a herbal sleep aid. When combined with the root, ashwagandha, and the herb, brahmi, which both have stress-relieving benefits, this drink makes a great holistic nightcap. While brahmi is known as a brain tonic, promoting alertness and mental agility, its ability to create an overall balanced emotional state promotes restful sleep.

240ml/8fl oz/1 cup oat milk, preferably homemade (see page 30)
1 tsp Wunder Instantly Golden Chai Latte Blend (or see right)
1 heaped tsp coconut oil
¼ tsp brahmi powder
¼ tsp ashwagandha root powder
¼ tsp valerian root powder
raw honey, to sweeten (optional)

Gently heat the milk in a small pan. Add the other ingredients, except for the honey, and heat until the milk almost reaches the boil, whisking continuously until frothy. (If you have a milk steamer, add all of the ingredients together and steam until hot and frothy.)

Pour into a mug and sweeten with raw honey, if you like. Add the honey to the mug, rather than the boiling milk in the pan to preserve its health benefits.

Homemade Instantly Golden Chai Latte Blend
If you don't have our Wunder Instantly Golden Chai, you can make your own version by blending equal amounts of turmeric powder, ground cinnamon, ground ginger, ground cardamom and a pinch of black pepper.

Super Root Cacao Ceremony

Prep and cook: 10 minutes
Serves: 1

Traditionally, cacao ceremonies were a sacred, ancient ritual of the Aztec and Mayan cultures. They were a celebration of the cacao bean's healing and heart-opening qualities. This recipe uses half the usual amount of raw cacao for a more gentle introduction to this endorphin-boosting bean. If this floats your boat, there are Shaman-led cacao ceremonies, remaining true to the traditional concept, now practised in most major cities.

1 tbsp ceremonial raw cacao powder or grated raw cacao

125ml/4½fl oz/½ cup hot water

pinch of chilli or cayenne powder

½ tsp ground ginger

1 tsp maca powder

½ tsp suma powder

½ tsp ground cinnamon

pinch of sea salt

1 tsp coconut syrup or raw honey, to sweeten (optional)

Add the cacao to a mug and cover with just enough hot water to create a thick paste, give the cacao a moment to dissolve, then stir well.

In a separate bowl, mix all the powdered ingredients together and add to the paste. Pour in the remaining hot water and stir well. The taste can be bitter, so sweeten with coconut syrup or honey.

Pour into a small cup and drink right away. This is usually a short drink, although you can make it longer by adding warmed plant-based milk.

Tonics

Wunder Morning Routine

Prep: 10 minutes
Serves: 1

Our Wunder morning routine has been a process of trial
and error, but we now see this as our most important
'meal' of the day. We are big fans of apple cider vinegar,
which has long been known for its therapeutic
properties. It is a gentle detoxifier, aids metabolism
and is a source of amino acids. The acetic acid in apple
cider vinegar not only boosts the immune system, it is
also an effective antiseptic and antibiotic. It's important
to buy a good-quality raw, unfiltered brand if you can.

1 tsp fresh turmeric juice
(about 3cm/1¼ inch piece
of fresh turmeric root),
or ½ tsp turmeric powder

1 tsp ginger juice (about 2cm/
¾ inch piece of fresh root ginger)

1 tbsp lemon juice

1 tbsp raw, unfiltered apple
cider vinegar

pinch of black pepper

60ml/2fl oz/¼ cup water

sweetener to taste, preferably raw
honey or date syrup

Put the turmeric, ginger, lemon juice and apple cider
vinegar into a mug. Add a pinch of pepper (only a
very small amount of black pepper is needed as it
can be really powerful and overwhelming if you use
too much).

Fill a quarter of the mug with cold water, then top up
with hot water so that the water is just warm. This is
important to preserve the benefits of the apple cider
vinegar. Stir well and serve.

Add a little sweetener if desired.

Ginseng Root Tea

Prep and cook: 20 minutes
Serves: 1–4

This combination of roots is used in Traditional Chinese Medicine and is prescribed as a tonic to rejuvenate and enhance the digestive, circulatory and immune systems. While you can also use other types of ginseng, Asian panax ginseng has been found to be the most potent as it contains high concentrations of ginsenosides. These have been shown to help prevent and treat inflammation-related illnesses. It is also a good soothing tonic for menstrual pain.

5g/⅛oz dried Asian panax ginseng root
10g/¼oz dried liquorice root
10g/¼oz nettle root powder
1 litre/35fl oz/4¼ cups water

Put all the ingredients in a pan and slowly bring to the boil. Turn the heat down and simmer for 15 minutes.

Strain the tea and pour into a cup(s). For the best results, drink four cups over the course of a day – either reheat or enjoy the tea cold.

Double Espresso
(The Wunder Way)

Prep: 15 minutes, plus soaking overnight
Serves: 1

When you've got a busy schedule ahead or are feeling tired, a shot of this double-power espresso is sure to fire you up. The fresh hazelnut milk is the perfect creamy alternative to milk and will help to sustain the caffeine buzz for longer, while the cordyceps (mushrooms used in Traditional Chinese Medicine) are known to help improve endurance and fight mental fatigue. Combining coffee with tonic herbs has a synergistic effect – the coffee helps the body to utilize the benefits of the tonic herbs more effectively and vice versa – supercharging your body and without the usual caffeine crash.

100g/3½oz/generous ¾ cup blanched hazelnuts
pinch of sea salt
1 drop vanilla extract
240ml/8fl oz/1 cup water
¼ tsp marshmallow root powder
½ tsp ground ginger
½ tsp ground cinnamon
¼ tsp cordyceps powder
1 shot freshly made espresso
sweetener to taste, preferably coconut blossom nectar (optional)

Soak the hazelnuts overnight in water. The next day, drain and rinse the nuts.

Put the soaked hazelnuts, salt and vanilla extract in a blender. Add the measured water, then blend until smooth and creamy. Strain the mixture through a nut milk bag or sieve lined with muslin (cheesecloth). (The nut pulp can be used to sprinkle over granola or yogurt.)

Pour the hazelnut milk into a pan and add the marshmallow root, ginger, cinnamon and cordyceps powder. Warm over a gentle heat, whisking continuously until combined and frothy. (If you have a milk steamer, add all of the ingredients together and steam until hot and frothy.)

Pour the espresso into a mug and top with the warm, frothy milk. Sweeten to taste, if you like.

Super Root Cold Brew

**Prep: 10 minutes, plus
12–18 hours infusing
Serves: 4**

Cold-brewed coffee is less acidic than regular hot coffee. When blending coffee with other ingredients, we would always recommend using cold brew as it allows more of the flavour of the ingredients to come through and adds its own natural sweetness. This super root cold brew has an Indian twist and is a great way to spice up your usual cup of coffee. What's more, coffee synergizes with the active compounds in turmeric and ginger, aiding the absorption of their beneficial compounds.

35g/1¼oz/1¼ tbsp coarsely ground coffee beans, preferably freshly ground

1 small cinnamon stick, roughly chopped

1 tsp ground cardamom seeds

15g/½oz piece of fresh turmeric root, finely chopped

30g/1oz piece of fresh root ginger, finely chopped

1 star anise

½ tsp ground nutmeg

pinch of black pepper

1 litre/35fl oz/4¼ cups filtered water or still mineral water

sweetener to taste, preferably coconut blossom nectar (optional)

ice cubes

Put all the ingredients, except the sweetener and ice, in a large glass bottle or jar. Leave in the refrigerator overnight or for 12–18 hours.

When ready to drink, filter the cold brew through a coffee filter and serve in mugs. Sweeten to taste, if you like, and serve with ice.

Ginger Switzel

Prep: 10 minutes, plus chilling overnight
Serves: 4

An age-old classic, switzels (or switchels) are vinegar-based health tonics that have been drunk for hundreds of years and are especially good for the gut. In this version, apple cider vinegar helps to regulate blood sugar and maintain energy levels, while sage is reported to improve cognitive function and memory, and may even aid those with Alzheimer's. Prepare the tonic on a Sunday evening for the week ahead and they'll be no more bleary-eyed starts to the day.

1 litre/35fl oz/4¼ cups water

1 tbsp Golden Spoon Turmeric Honey (Wunder Workshop or see page 92)

8cm/3¼ inch piece of fresh root ginger, finely chopped

4cm/1½ inch piece of fresh galangal root, finely chopped

6 sage leaves, plus extra to serve (optional)

4 tbsp raw, unfiltered apple cider vinegar

ice cubes

Heat 240ml/8fl oz/1 cup of the water in a pan until warm, then stir in the Golden Spoon Turmeric Honey until melted. Pour it into a jug.

Add the ginger, galangal, sage, apple cider vinegar and the remaining water into the jug, stir and chill in the refrigerator overnight.

Stir then strain through a sieve before serving with extra sage leaves, if using, and ice.

Kashaya

Prep and cook: 15 minutes
Serves: 2

Kashaya is an Ayurvedic drink that comes in many variations but is traditionally based on five key spices – turmeric, fennel seeds, coriander seeds, cumin seeds and black pepper – that have been used for thousands of years to boost the immune system and aid digestion. We use this recipe for a real immune-boosting lift and it's a go-to if there's even a hint of a tickle in the throat or a cough coming on. The spice roots will help to elevate the beneficial effects of the spices and add a warming, fiery taste.

50g/1¾oz dried ashwagandha root pieces
2cm/¾ inch piece of liquorice root or 1 tsp powder
1 tbsp grated fresh root ginger
2 cloves
500ml/17fl oz/2 cups plant-based milk (we think coconut works best in this recipe)

Spice base:
1 tbsp turmeric powder
2 tsp fennel seeds
2 tsp cumin seeds
2 tsp coriander seeds
1 tsp black peppercorns

To make the spice base, put the turmeric powder, fennel seeds, cumin seeds, coriander seeds and black peppercorns in a large, dry frying pan and heat over a medium-low heat for 2 minutes until you can smell the aroma of the spices.

Grind the toasted spices into a fine powder using a pestle and mortar or spice grinder – this can then be used straightaway or left to cool and stored in an airtight container for up to 2 weeks.

To make the kashaya, put the ashwagandha root, liquorice, ginger, cloves and plant-based milk in a saucepan. Add 2 teaspoons of the spice base mix to the pan and gently warm to just below boiling point, about 5 minutes.

Strain through a sieve and serve warm in mugs or heatproof glasses.

Amazonian Aphrodisiac

Prep and cook: 15 minutes
Serves: 2

This is a tonic as wild and wonderful as the Amazon itself. The amazing collection of roots are renowned in South America for their aphrodisiac and stimulating properties, so handle with care and in the right company! Muira puama, often called 'potency wood', is believed to boost sexual health, while suma (Brazilian ginseng) is an adaptogen and is often referred to as 'para toda' (meaning 'for all things') thanks to its normalizing and stress-reducing properties. Pau d'arco is an Amazonian wonder that comes from the inner bark of the Lapacho tree, the Paraguayan national tree. It is readily available and makes a uniquely fragrant tea. Lucuma is a fruit native to Peru and has a taste similar to caramel. It is often used as a natural sweetener, due to its low glycaemic index.

1 tbsp muira puama root or
1 tsp powder
1 tbsp suma root or 1 tsp powder
1 tsp lucuma powder
1 tsp pau d'arco tea
450ml/16fl oz/scant 2 cups water

Put all the ingredients in a pan and stir well. Bring to the boil then turn the heat down and simmer for 10 minutes.

Strain through a sieve into two mugs. Enjoy!

Good Night Hug

Prep and cook: 15 minutes
Serves: 1

A calming and sleep-promoting blend of roots and spices that makes a perfect night-time drink – just like that comforting feeling of being tucked up in bed.

1 tsp dried burdock root

1 tsp dried ashwagandha root pieces or ½ tsp powder

1 tsp dried valerian root pieces

1 tsp dried lemongrass leaves

¼ tsp ground nutmeg

4cm/1½ inch piece of fresh root ginger, chopped

300ml/10½fl oz/1¼ cups water

Put all the ingredients in a pan and stir well until combined. Bring to the boil, then turn the heat down and simmer for 10 minutes.

Strain through a sieve into a mug and serve.

Bites

Golden Turmeric Granola

Prep and cook: 50 minutes
Serves: 4

Sprinkle over yogurt, add to a smoothie bowl or eat as a snack, granola is a versatile and easy way to incorporate the wonders of turmeric into your diet. It's worth making a double batch to store in a Kilner jar for whenever you need it. The granola will keep for a couple of weeks – if it lasts that long!

1 tbsp coconut oil

1 tsp turmeric powder

½ tsp ground cinnamon

60g/2¼oz/scant ½ cup porridge oats (oatmeal)

1 fresh raw beetroot (beet), grated

2cm/¾ inch piece of fresh root ginger, grated

1 tbsp almonds, roughly chopped

1 tbsp walnut pieces, roughly chopped

2 dried soft pitted dates, roughly chopped

1 tbsp coconut syrup or runny honey

Preheat the oven to 100°C/200°F/gas ¼ and line a large baking pan with parchment paper.

Melt the coconut oil in a large frying pan, then stir in the turmeric and cinnamon until mixed with the oil.

Remove the pan from the heat, add the oats and stir until coated in the turmeric and cinnamon oil.

Stir in the beetroot, ginger, nuts and dates before drizzling the coconut syrup or honey evenly over the mixture. Stir well until combined.

Tip the granola mixture onto the lined baking pan and spread out evenly. Bake for 30 minutes until golden and crisp, turning the mixture halfway through to make sure it cooks evenly and doesn't stick. Leave to cool before serving.

Buckwheat & Root Pancakes

Prep and cook: 30 minutes
Makes: 8

When it comes to pancakes, we like to supercharge the batter with ashwagandha, commonly used in Ayurvedic eating for its stress-reducing adaptogenic properties, and burdock for preventing blood glucose spikes, a frequent consequence of eating pancakes (depending on which toppings you choose!). These American-style, fluffy pancakes are great for sharing.

125g/4½oz/scant 1 cup buckwheat flour
½ tsp gluten-free baking powder
½ tsp gluten-free bicarbonate of soda (baking soda)
pinch of salt
125ml/4½fl oz/½ cup plant milk, any type will do
1 tsp turmeric powder
1 tsp ashwagandha root powder
½ tsp burdock root powder
2–3 tbsp maple syrup
coconut oil, for frying
fresh berries and maple syrup, to serve

To make the pancakes, mix together the buckwheat flour, baking powder, bicarbonate of soda and salt in a large mixing bowl.

Warm the plant milk in a small saucepan and stir in the turmeric, ashwagandha, burdock root powder and maple syrup.

Mix the wet ingredients into the flour mixture and stir until you have a smooth, thick batter. Add more plant milk, if necessary. Leave to rest for 10 minutes.

Heat a large frying pan over a medium heat and add a little coconut oil to lightly coat the surface. Place 2 tablespoons of the batter into the pan per pancake and form into an even circle. Cook for 2 minutes until the bottom is set and light golden, then flip over and cook for another 2 minutes. You should have enough batter to make 8 small pancakes.

Serve with fresh berries, drizzled with maple syrup.

Turmeric Flatbreads

**Prep and cook: 1 hour,
plus resting
Makes: 4**

Flatbreads are the simplest type of bread to make, requiring little planning, no yeast, just flour, milk, oil and, in this case, spice roots. Adding a little bit of effort and (almost) breaking a sweat when cooking always fires up the appetite, so take time to knead the dough into a smooth ball for best results.

300g/10½oz/2½ cups plain (all-purpose) flour, plus extra for dusting

1 teaspoon turmeric powder

½ tsp sea salt

pinch of black pepper

175ml/6fl oz/¾ cup plant milk, such as oat or almond

50g/1¾oz coconut oil, plus extra for frying

Mix together the flour, turmeric, salt and pepper in a large mixing bowl.

Gently heat the plant milk and coconut oil in a small pan until the coconut oil melts, then stir until combined. Pour the wet ingredients into the flour mixture and mix well, first with a fork then with your hands, until combined into a dough. (You may wish to wear plastic gloves to avoid yellow turmeric hands.)

Tip the dough onto a lightly floured work surface and knead for 8–10 minutes until you have a smooth, firm ball of dough. Return the dough to the bowl, cover and leave to rest for 30 minutes.

Lightly dust the work surface with flour. Cut the dough into 4 equal pieces and roll out each one into a thin flat round.

Heat a large frying pan over a high heat and add a little coconut oil to lightly coat the base. Place one of the flatbreads in the pan and cook for 4 minutes on each side or until golden. Keep warm while you cook the remaining flatbreads. They are best served warm.

Golden Spiced Sourdough

**Prep and cook: 1½ hours, plus
24 hours starter preparation
and 2 days rising/proving
Makes: 1 loaf**

Baking bread has always been a favourite for Tom and we both agree there's nothing better than the smell and warmth that it brings to the kitchen. The key to this recipe is the sourdough or 'wild-harvested' starter, which takes a bit of time and dedication to get going but, be patient, it is worth the wait for both the flavour and digestive benefits it gives the bread.

150g/5½oz/1½cups
organic rye flour
150ml/5fl oz/scant ⅔ cup water

First make the sourdough starter:
Put 50g/1¾oz/½ cup of the organic rye flour and 50ml/2fl oz/¼ cup of the water in a large jar and mix well. Set aside for 8 hours at room temperature, leaving the lid ajar to allow the release of any gases that build up.

Continue to add equal parts of flour and water to the jar at regular 8-hourly intervals until used up. The starter will expand with time, bubbles will appear on the surface and it should have a slightly fruity fragrance when ready to use.

You are now ready to prepare the bread...

(Continued overleaf)

350ml/12fl oz/1½ cups water

2 tsp turmeric powder

150g/5½oz/1½ cups organic rye sourdough starter (see page 63)

350g/12oz/rounded 2½ cups organic strong white flour (white bread flour), plus extra for dusting

150g/5½oz/heaped 1 cup organic strong wholemeal flour (wholewheat bread flour)

10g/¼oz sea salt (we like Pink Himalayan)

1 tbsp cumin seeds

1 tbsp coriander seeds

½ tsp freshly ground black pepper

Day 1:

Combine the water, turmeric and sourdough starter in a mixing bowl.

Mix the white flour, wholemeal flour and salt in a separate large mixing bowl and make a well in the middle. Add the wet ingredients to the dry ingredients and mix them together with a fork to make a loose dough.

Tip the dough out of the bowl onto a lightly floured work surface and knead for 10 minutes or until it forms a smooth, elastic ball of dough – it should spring back when pressed. (You may wish to wear plastic gloves to avoid yellow turmeric hands.)

Return the dough to the cleaned mixing bowl, cover and leave to slowly rise in the refrigerator for 12–18 hours until almost doubled in size. This slow rise allows the flavour of the bread to develop.

Day 2:

Very loosely crush the cumin and coriander seeds then mix with the ground black pepper. Remove the dough from the refrigerator, turn out onto a floured work surface, and fold the spices into the dough. The best way to do this is to add a quarter of the spices, then pull one side of the dough up from the bottom to the top, stretching it over to the opposite side. Repeat this folding process four times until all the spices are added and evenly incorporated into the dough.

Put the dough back in the bowl, cover the bowl with a clean towel or cling film (plastic wrap) and leave to rest for 30 minutes, before repeating the folding process again. Leave to rest for a further 10 minutes before placing the dough in a generously floured proving basket. Leave it to rise in a warm, draught-free place for 1 hour until doubled in size.

Preheat the oven to 200°C/400°F/gas 6.

Carefully turn the dough out of the proving basket onto a lightly floured baking sheet, then score the top a few times with a sharp knife.

Bake the bread for 30 minutes, turning it 180 degrees halfway through the cooking time, until risen and golden. To check that the bread is fully cooked, tap the bottom – it should sound hollow when ready. Leave to rest and cool for 30 minutes before serving.

Turmeric Cauli Pizza

Prep and cook: 1 hour
Serves: 2

This healthy, low-carb and gluten-free pizza has a satisfying crisp, golden cauliflower base. Make sure to cook the base separately before getting creative with your toppings.

1 tbsp melted coconut oil, for greasing
500g/1lb 2oz cauliflower florets, roughly chopped
1 red onion, diced
2 garlic cloves, finely chopped
10g/¼oz piece of fresh turmeric root, diced
200ml/7fl oz/scant 1 cup water
1 egg, lightly beaten
sea salt and black pepper

Toppings:

100g/3½oz feta cheese, crumbled
1 fresh raw beetroot (beet), grated
50g/1¾oz/½ cup chopped walnuts
6 tbsp tomato sauce
1-2 eggs
1 handful of spinach leaves
Parmesan cheese, finely grated
basil leaves

Preheat the oven to 180°C/350°F/gas 4. Line a large baking sheet with parchment paper and lightly grease the paper with coconut oil.

Add the cauliflower, onion, garlic and turmeric to a food processor and pulse until you have fine cauliflower 'dough' or paste. Bring the water to the boil in a saucepan, then add the cauliflower mixture. Turn the heat down and cook for 5 minutes until soft.

Drain the cauliflower mixture well through a sieve and place in a mixing bowl. Mix in the egg until combined. Season with salt and pepper. Spread the mixture out over the lightly oiled parchment paper to make an even pizza base, about 1cm/½ inch thick. You can make the edges slightly thicker for that pizza crust look.

Bake the base in the preheated oven for 30 minutes until crisp and golden.

Now add your toppings – we love feta with beetroot and walnuts for a sweet/savoury taste. Alternatively, try tomato and spinach with an egg cracked on top. Drizzle with olive oil and bake for a further 5 minutes until cooked through. Finish with more olive oil, black pepper, grated Parmesan and basil.

Super Root Veggie Burgers

**Prep and cook: 40 minutes,
plus chilling
Serves: 4**

Veggie burgers are a wonderfully nutritious way to satisfy hunger pangs. Black beans are packed full of protein, which makes them a great plant-based substitute for meat. We like to top the burgers with a spoonful of our Turmeric, Tamarind, Date and Ginger Chutney (see page 95) for a sweet Indian touch.

1 tbsp coconut oil, plus extra
for frying
1 onion, finely chopped
3cm/1¼ inch piece of galangal
root, minced
2 garlic cloves, finely chopped
½ tsp ground cumin
1 tsp ground coriander
1 tbsp tomato paste
400g/14oz can black beans,
drained and rinsed
1 egg, lightly beaten
½ tsp Himalayan sea salt
80g/2¾oz/heaped ½ cup
oat flour

Heat the oil in a large frying pan, add the onion and fry for 5 minutes until soft. Add the galangal, garlic, cumin, coriander and tomato paste and cook for a further minute. Add the black beans to the pan and heat through thoroughly, stirring occasionally. When warm, tip everything into a heatproof mixing bowl.

Add the egg and salt to the bowl, then mash well with a potato masher to crush the beans – the mixture should be quite loose. Add the oat flour and stir to make a slightly sticky, but not crumbly mixture.

Shape the mixture into 4 burger patties with floured hands and place in the refrigerator for 30 minutes to allow the burgers to firm up.

To serve:

4 lightly toasted burger buns, split
in half, or Turmeric Flatbreads
(see page 61)
crisp lettuce leaves
beefsteak tomato, sliced
Turmeric, Tamarind, Date and
Ginger Chutney (see page 95)

Wipe clean the frying pan, add enough coconut oil to coat the base of the pan and heat over a medium heat. Add the burgers and cook for 5–6 minutes on each side until golden and crisp on the outside and heated through.

Serve each burger in a bun (or on a turmeric flatbread) with lettuce leaves, tomato and a spoonful of chutney.

Golden Chickpea Crunchies

Prep and cook: 50 minutes
Serves: 4

These chickpea crunchies make a healthy, moreish snack and are delicious with a hint of Indian spice. The turmeric turns them a wonderful colour, but be wary of golden fingers. They also make a great topping for salads or savoury bowls. Peeling off the skins of the chickpeas can seem like an arduous task but it is worth it for removing extra lectins – plant proteins that can cause inflammation – produced by the skins. It is also strangely therapeutic!

500g/1lb 2oz canned chickpeas (garbanzo beans), drained and rinsed
2 tbsp olive oil
1 tsp turmeric powder
½ tsp ground coriander
½ tsp ground cumin
¼ tsp cayenne pepper
½ tsp sea salt
pinch of black pepper

To serve (optional):
mixed green salad leaves
Root Spiced Salad Dressing (see page 93)

Preheat the oven to 180°C/350°F/gas 4. Line 2 large baking pans with parchment paper.

Dry the chickpeas well with paper towels, rubbing off the skins if preferred.

Mix the olive oil, spices, salt and pepper in a large mixing bowl. Add the chickpeas and turn them until coated in the spice oil.

Tip the chickpeas onto the baking pans and spread out evenly. Roast for 40 minutes, occasionally shaking the pans to make sure the chickpeas cook evenly, until golden and crisp. Leave to cool and crisp up further.

Serve the chickpeas as a snack or scattered over a green leaf salad with the root spiced salad dressing.

Turmeric Kraut

**Prep: 20 minutes, plus
5–7 days fermentation
Makes about: 400g/14oz**

Sauerkraut is packed full of beneficial bacteria and is celebrated for its gut-supporting, antiviral and anti-inflammatory qualities. If this is your first sauerkraut, we recommend starting with a 5–7 day fermentation period and then increasing it by a week each time you make it. Apparently, bacterial levels peak at 21 days, but its taste won't be for the faint hearted!

1 small white cabbage, finely sliced (1 outer leaf reserved)

1½ tsp sea salt

2cm/¾ inch piece of fresh root ginger, cut into small pieces

1cm/½ inch piece of fresh turmeric root, finely chopped or ½ tsp turmeric powder

¼ tsp cumin seeds

1cm/½ inch piece of fresh galangal root, finely chopped

¼ red onion, finely sliced

1 garlic clove, cut into small pieces

Place the cabbage in a mixing bowl with the salt and knead well with your hands for about 5 minutes to make a brine. (The salt helps to draw out any liquid in the cabbage.) Stir in the remaining ingredients.

Spoon the cabbage mixture into a sterilized 1 litre/35fl oz/4 cup lidded jar, then pour in the brine from the bowl. Press the cabbage mixture down as much as possible to submerge it in the brine. If there isn't enough liquid, pour in some filtered water until everything is covered. Place the reserved cabbage leaf on top. If there is space at the top of the jar, it is a good idea to top the cabbage leaf with a weight, to keep everything submerged and to prevent oxidation.

Sterilizing jars

It is important to sterilize your jar before use: first wash the jar in hot, soapy water. Rinse well. Place on a baking sheet in a preheated oven at 120°C/240°F/Gas ½ for 15 minutes. Leave the jar to cool before use.

Loosely cover the jar with a coffee filter or a piece of muslin (cheesecloth) and secure with an elastic band. Leave in a dark place at a cool room temperature for 5–7 days. It will be ready to eat after 5 days but leaving if for longer will give a stronger flavour. Check the cabbage every day or so to make sure it hasn't spoiled and to release any gases that may have built up, then replace the cover. When you are happy with the flavour, cover the jar with a lid. It is ready to eat but will keep in the refrigerator for a few months.

73

Bowls

Golden Booster Bowl

Prep: 15 minutes
Serves: 1

Sweet potato is delicious in both sweet and savoury dishes and this healthy breakfast bowl is no exception. It's a good idea to plan ahead and bake an extra sweet potato or two the night before to save you time in the morning.

1½ tbsp whole linseeds (flaxseeds) or 1 tbsp ground

200g/7oz cooked, cooled sweet potato, skin removed, lightly mashed

¼ tsp turmeric powder

½ tsp Siberian ginseng powder

pinch of black pepper

1 tbsp coconut butter, such as Coconut Manna

¼ tsp ground cinnamon

¼ tsp ground ginger

1 tsp maca powder

150ml/5fl oz/scant ⅔ cup unsweetened almond milk

½ banana

Toppings – choose from:

shelled hemp seeds, walnuts, almonds, cacao nibs, bee pollen, desiccated (shredded) coconut, fresh berries and/or Golden Turmeric Granola (see page 59)

If using whole linseeds, grind them in a mini food processor or grinder (it's always best to use freshly ground linseeds as they have a greater nutritional value than ready-ground ones).

Put the sweet potato, ground linseeds and all the other ingredients in a blender and blend well.

Pour or spoon into a bowl and add your choice of toppings – we like the crunchiness of brain-boosting walnuts and hemp seeds for creaminess and protein. Fresh berries, chopped almonds, cacao nibs and granola are good too.

Immune-boosting Congee

Prep and cook:
1 hour 20 minutes
Serves: 4

This Asian savoury rice porridge or congee is perfect for supporting your immune system. It's also beautifully warming, hearty and loaded with beneficial super roots like astragalus and Siberian ginseng, which will both help to boost your resistance to colds and flu. If the astragalus root is still tough and chewy after slow-cooking, do remove it before serving. Placing it first in a muslin (cheesecloth) bag, similar to a bouquet garni, makes it so much easier to take out at the end of cooking.

1.25 litre/40fl oz/5 cups water

100g/3½oz/½ cup short grain brown rice

20g/¾oz dried astragalus root pieces

2 tsp Siberian ginseng powder

2 tbsp coconut oil

1 onion, thinly sliced

300g/10½oz shiitake mushrooms, sliced

3cm/1¼ inch piece of fresh root ginger, minced

2 garlic cloves, minced

2 tbsp brown (genmai) miso paste

4 pak choi (bok choy), halved lengthways

2 tsp sesame oil

black pepper

Pour the water into a pan and add the rice, astragalus and Siberian ginseng. Stir and bring to the boil then turn the heat down, cover and simmer for 1 hour until the rice is very tender. Remove from the heat.

Heat the coconut oil in a large frying pan over a medium heat. Add the onion and fry for 3 minutes. Add the shiitake mushrooms, ginger and garlic and sauté for 3 minutes before adding to the congee. Simmer for 10 minutes, stirring often to prevent it sticking to the base of the pan.

Use a little of the congee water to dissolve the miso paste then stir it into the congee with the pak choi and sesame oil. Let the congee simmer for a further 3 minutes before serving in bowls. Season with black pepper.

Creamy Golden Mushrooms

Prep and cook: 20 minutes
Serves: 2

These wholesome, meaty mushrooms in a creamy, dairy-free sauce make a simple and satisfying meal – perfect with rice or spaghetti. For an extra mushroomy flavour, try adding ½ teaspoon reishi powder.

1 tbsp coconut oil

2 garlic cloves, minced

2cm/¾ inch piece of fresh turmeric root, finely chopped

½ tsp black onion seeds

125g/4½oz shiitake mushrooms, sliced

100g/3½oz fresh wild mushrooms, sliced

200ml/7fl oz/scant 1 cup almond cream

sea salt and black pepper

cooked wholegrain spaghetti or brown rice, to serve

Melt the coconut oil in a large frying pan over a medium heat. Add the garlic, turmeric and black onion seeds and fry for 1 minute, stirring.

Add all of the mushrooms and fry for 4 minutes until soft and golden brown.

Turn the heat down and add the almond cream. Season with salt and pepper, then simmer for 5 minutes, stirring, until heated through. Serve in bowls with rice or spaghetti.

Prep and cook: 50 minutes
Serves: 4

Burdock & Mushroom Stir-fry with Horseradish Mash

2 x 15cm/6 inch pieces of fresh burdock root, cut into matchsticks

2 tbsp white wine vinegar

100ml/3½fl oz/scant ½ cup sake

4 tbsp sweet soy sauce

2 tbsp toasted sesame oil

2 tbsp coconut oil

1 onion, sliced

1 garlic clove, minced

2cm/¾ inch piece of fresh root ginger, finely chopped

300g/10½oz oyster mushrooms, sliced

flat-leaf parsley, to garnish

Horseradish mash:

6 white potatoes, peeled and halved (or quartered if large)

2 garlic cloves, finely chopped

4cm/1½ inch piece of fresh horseradish root, peeled and roughly chopped

2 tbsp white wine vinegar

1 tbsp water

3 tbsp olive oil

sea salt and black pepper

Fresh burdock root has a distinct crisp texture and makes a great addition to stir-fries. To retain its crunch, soak it in water and vinegar before use. You could use 1 tablespoon horseradish sauce if more convenient than the fresh root.

To make the horseradish mash, boil the potatoes for 20 minutes or until tender. Add the garlic about 5 minutes before the potatoes are ready.

Meanwhile, start preparing the stir-fry. Put the burdock root in a bowl of water with the white wine vinegar, stir and leave to sit for 15 minutes. Mix together the sake, soy sauce and sesame oil in a small bowl and set aside. Back to the mash: put the horseradish root in a mini food processor with the vinegar and water and a pinch of salt. Blitz until the root is very finely chopped. Set aside.

Drain the potatoes well and let them dry in the heat of the pan, then add the olive oil and horseradish mixture. Mash the potatoes until smooth. Season with salt and pepper to taste. Cover and set aside.

Heat the coconut oil in a wok or frying pan over a high heat. Add the onion and stir-fry for 5 minutes. Add the garlic and ginger and stir-fry for 30 seconds before adding the mushrooms. Drain the burdock root and add to the pan. Stir-fry until the mushrooms are golden, about 5 minutes. Add the sake mixture and toss until heated through. Spoon the mash and stir-fry into bowls and garnish with parsley.

Black Bean Fo-ti with Turmeric Flatbreads

Prep and cook: 30 minutes
Serves: 4

Black beans bring out the best in fo-ti (he shou wu), a highly esteemed super root herb used in Traditional Chinese Medicine. Combining the two ingredients, a method described as far back as the Tang Dynasty (618–907 CE), is considered the best way to attain the immune-boosting and antioxidant benefits of the fo-ti. We have incorporated this ancient wisdom into a more modern recipe with a Mexican twist.

2 tbsp coconut oil
1 onion, chopped
2 garlic cloves, minced
1 tbsp tomato purée (paste)
½ tsp cayenne pepper
400g/14oz can black beans, drained and rinsed
1 tsp fo-ti root powder
2 tsp whole coriander seeds
½ tsp ground cumin
2 tomatoes, roughly chopped
juice of 1 lime
sea salt and black pepper
fresh coriander (cilantro) leaves and watercress, to garnish
Turmeric Flatbreads (see page 61), to serve

Heat the coconut oil in a large frying pan with a lid over a medium heat. Add the onion and fry for 5 minutes until soft and starting to colour.

Add the garlic, tomato purée and cayenne pepper and fry for 1 minute, stirring, before adding the black beans, fo-ti powder, coriander seeds, cumin and tomatoes. (We like to use whole coriander seeds for their intense burst of flavour, but you can crush them or use ground if preferred.)

Cover the pan and simmer for 8 minutes, stirring frequently so the beans do not stick. If the beans begin to look dry, stir in a little water. When the beans are ready, squeeze in the lime juice and season with salt and pepper.

Scatter the coriander leaves and watercress over the black beans and serve with the flatbreads. (The beans are also delicious with rice.)

Tom's Jackfruit Curry

Prep and cook: 40 minutes
Serves: 2

There's nothing better than a warming bowl of curry and this recipe is so easy to make. Jackfruit is the perfect vegetarian substitute for tender, slow-cooked meat. Our advice would be to cook more than you need since the curry almost tastes better the next day when the spices have had time to meld with the jackfruit and chickpeas.

2 tbsp coconut oil
1 tsp yellow mustard seeds
1 tsp cumin seeds
1 onion, finely diced
1 tsp minced fresh turmeric root
3 garlic cloves, minced
1 tsp minced fresh root ginger
½ tsp minced fresh galangal root
1 tbsp tomato purée (paste)
2 tsp ground cumin
1 tsp ground coriander
½ tsp chilli powder
400g/14oz can chickpeas (garbanzo beans), drained and rinsed
400g/14oz can jackfruit, drained and rinsed
3 tbsp water
sea salt and black pepper
Turmeric Flatbreads (see page 61), rice, lime wedges and yogurt, to serve
coriander (cilantro) leaves, to garnish

Heat the coconut oil in a large, heavy saucepan until melted, then add the yellow mustard seeds. When they begin to pop, add the cumin seeds and onion and cook for a further 5 minutes until the onion is soft and starts to colour.

Add the turmeric, garlic, ginger and galangal along with the tomato purée, ground cumin, coriander and chilli and fry for 1 minute, stirring well.

Add the chickpeas, jackfruit and water, then cover with a lid and simmer over a medium-low heat for 10 minutes, stirring occasionally to make sure the curry doesn't stick to the base of the pan. Add more water if the curry begins to dry out – it should be reasonably thick in consistency. I like to slightly crush the chunks with the back of a fork so that the jackfruit is able to absorb the flavour of the spices. Season to taste with salt and pepper.

Serve with flatbreads, rice, lime wedges and yogurt (you could also grate over a little lime zest) and garnish with coriander leaves.

Gold & Black Rice Bowl

Prep and cook: 1 hour
Serves: 4

This black rice bowl is a bit of a showstopper and can be served hot or cold. Not only is black rice nutritious, the colour contrast with the turmeric tofu and edamame beans is stunning. It makes a great picnic dish since it's simple to prepare and holds up well when transported.

125g/4½oz/¾ cup black rice, washed

240ml/8fl oz/1 cup water

50g/1¾oz/½ cup cashew nuts

1 tbsp sesame seeds

2 tbsp coconut oil

2cm/¾ inch piece of fresh turmeric root, finely chopped

3cm/1¼ inch piece of fresh root ginger, minced

1 tsp dried chilli flakes

200g/7oz firm tofu, drained well, patted dry and cut into 1cm/½ inch cubes

100g/3½oz/scant 1 cup frozen edamame (soya) beans

3 tbsp pomegranate seeds

2 tbsp sesame oil

pinch of black pepper

2 tbsp tamari

fresh coriander (cilantro) leaves, to garnish

Put the black rice in a pan with the water and bring to the boil. Turn the heat down to its lowest setting and simmer, covered, until the rice is tender, about 35–40 minutes. Drain the rice, if needed.

While the rice is cooking, toast the cashews and sesame seeds in a large, dry frying pan for about 5 minutes until light brown, then set aside.

Ten minutes before the rice is ready, heat the coconut oil in the frying pan until melted. Add the turmeric and ginger and fry for 2 minutes.

Add the chilli flakes, tofu and edamame and fry for 5 minutes, stirring regularly, until the tofu is golden.

Add the black rice to the pan with the pomegranate seeds, sesame oil, pepper and tamari. Turn briefly until everything is mixed together, then spoon into serving bowls.

Scatter over the toasted sesame seeds and cashews and garnish with coriander. (Alternatively, place everything in separate serving bowls and let everyone help themselves.)

Coconut Cauli Cream Soup

Prep and cook: 40 minutes
Serves: 4

This warming soup is perfect for a cold winter's day. It's loaded with immune-boosting, wholesome nutrients thanks to a potent blend of super roots, including ashwagandha, ginger and burdock.

1 tbsp coconut oil
1 large garlic clove, chopped
1 tsp mustard seeds
1 tsp sea salt
1 onion, diced
1 litre/35fl oz/4¼ cups vegetable broth or stock
1 tsp ground ginger
½ tsp burdock root powder
1 tsp ashwagandha root powder
½ tsp ground nutmeg
1 cauliflower, cut into chunks
1 tbsp nutritional yeast flakes
200ml/7fl oz/scant 1 cup coconut milk
2 tsp black sesame seeds
sprouted amaranth, red micro leaves or cress, to garnish
black pepper

Heat the coconut oil in a large saucepan. Add the garlic, mustard seeds, salt and onion and cook for 5 minutes, stirring often, until the onion is soft.

Add the vegetable broth or stock with the ginger, burdock, ashwagandha and nutmeg. Stir until combined then add the cauliflower. Bring to the boil, then turn the heat down and simmer for 20 minutes or until the cauliflower is tender. Add the nutritional yeast flakes and coconut milk and heat through.

Using a hand blender, blend the soup until smooth.

Ladle the soup into bowls and garnish with black sesame seeds, amaranth, red micro leaves or cress, and season with black pepper.

Super Bowl

Prep and cook: 50 minutes
Serves: 2

This is one of our favourite nurturing bowls – a powerhouse of nutrients with a satisfying umami flavour.

20g/¾oz dried astragalus root pieces

20g/¾oz dried burdock root pieces

10g/½oz fresh root ginger, chopped

1 tbsp barley miso paste

1 tsp chilli flakes

1.2 litres/40fl oz/5 cups water

1 vegetable bouillon cube

140g/5oz/1 cup jumbo porridge oats (oatmeal)

150g/5½oz/1 cup pinhead oatmeal (steel-cut oats)

1 tbsp coconut oil

2 garlic cloves, finely chopped

100g/3½oz tempeh, cut into thin slices

1 tsp sesame oil

1 avocado, halved, stoned (pitted), peeled and sliced

1 handful of watercress leaves

red chilli sauce, to taste

sea salt and black pepper

Put all the roots, miso paste, chilli flakes and water in a large, heavy saucepan. Bring to the boil and stir in the vegetable bouillon cube until dissolved. Turn the heat down and simmer for 40 minutes to allow the roots to infuse and release their nurturing properties into the broth.

Let the broth cool a little and then strain through a sieve into a separate pan – there should be about 1 litre/35fl oz/4¼ cups. Add the oats and oatmeal and stir well. Simmer for 15 minutes, stirring often, until the oats are cooked.

In the meantime, heat the coconut oil in a large frying pan until melted and add the garlic and tempeh. Season with salt and pepper. Fry the tempeh until golden all over, about 8 minutes.

Serve the oats in bowls, arrange the tempeh on top and drizzle over the sesame oil. Top with the avocado and watercress, and add red chilli sauce, to taste.

Butters, Pastes & Dressings

Maca-Maca Nut Butter

Prep: 10 minutes
Makes about: 250g/
9oz/1 rounded cup

250g/9oz/2 cups
macadamia nuts
1 drop vanilla extract
pinch of sea salt
1 tsp coconut syrup
1 tsp maca powder
1 tsp shatavari root powder
1 heaped tsp coconut oil
½ tsp turmeric powder

Macadamia nuts are native to Zoë's birthplace, Australia, and grow in the hills around Queensland. They are a staple ingredient in our kitchen and give such a rich and creamy texture to homemade nut butters. For the best results, blend the nut butter until perfectly smooth as this brings out the sweetness of the maca. Spread this energizing butter on toast, add it to porridge or smoothies, or just spoon straight from the jar.

Place all the ingredients in a food processor and blend on a low speed for 4-5 minutes until smooth and creamy. If you prefer a crunchier nut butter, blend it for slightly less time. Spoon into a jar, cover and store in a cool, dry place.

Golden Almond Butter

Prep: 20 minutes
Makes about: 250g/
9oz/1 rounded cup

250g/9oz/2 cups
unblanched almonds
½ tsp turmeric powder
½ tsp garlic powder or 1 garlic
clove, minced
½ fresh red chilli, seeds removed

This is one of our favourite savoury nut butters to make. Spread it over warm sourdough bread or serve as a delicious satay sauce spooned on top of a rice bowl.

Put the almonds in a food processor and blitz on a high setting until smooth and creamy. Note, this can take at least 15 minutes! If the blended nuts start to stick to the sides, turn off the blender and push them back into the path of the blades.

Once smooth, add the turmeric, garlic powder (or fresh garlic) and chilli and blend briefly until combined. Spoon it into a jar, cover and store in the refrigerator for up to 1 week.

Golden Spoon Turmeric Honey

Prep: 10 minutes
Makes: 115g/4oz

A golden spoon a day is the perfect way to fight off colds and coughs. The antibacterial and antifungal properties of honey and turmeric help to soothe and heal minor ailments. Ashwagandha's ability to lower levels of cortisol, the stress hormone, will also enable the immune system to function more effectively. We recommend one teaspoon a day when you feel a sore throat or tickly cough coming on.

110g/3¾oz raw honey
1 tsp coconut oil
¾ tsp turmeric powder
pinch of ashwagandha root powder
pinch of black pepper

Pour the honey into a small sterilized jar (see page 72).

Gently warm the coconut oil in a pan until melted. Stir it into the honey.

Mix together the turmeric, ashwagandha and black pepper before stirring it into the honey mixture. It will keep for up to 1 month at room temperature.

Root Spiced Salad Dressing

Prep: 5 minutes
Makes: 5 tbsp

Loaded with the benefits of valerian and horseradish root, this salad dressing also features heart-friendly apple cider vinegar. The floral tones of the valerian make it a perfect addition to most salads, particularly those containing spicy leaves such as rocket or watercress. Valerian is renowned for its ability to relax and aid sleep. Horseradish is a natural antibiotic and helps to ward off common colds and flu, so this is a salad dressing that will boost your health in more ways than one.

1 tbsp extra-virgin olive oil
1 tbsp runny honey
3 tbsp raw, unfiltered apple cider vinegar
1 tsp valerian root powder
1 tsp horseradish root powder
pinch of black pepper
1 garlic clove, finely diced
juice of 1 lemon

Put all of the ingredients in a mixing bowl and whisk until well combined. Serve straightaway or store in a jar in the refrigerator for up to 1 week.

Garlic & Ginger Paste

Prep: 5 minutes

This is a must-have paste in many south-east Asian curries, but don't let that keep you from using it in other dishes such as stir-fries, soups and stews. No matter what cuisine, a spoonful of this garlic and ginger paste will bring it to life as well as enhance its health benefits. We recommend making a big batch – it will keep in the refrigerator for up to 1 week if stored in an airtight jar.

2 parts fresh garlic, finely diced
1 part fresh root ginger, finely diced

Grind the garlic and ginger into a paste using a pestle and mortar. If making a large quantity, put the garlic and ginger in a mini food processor and blend to a paste.

Spoon into a jar, cover and store in the refrigerator for up to 1 week.

Turmeric, Tamarind, Date & Ginger Chutney

Prep: 15 minutes
Makes about: 600g/1lb 5oz

This flavourful quick chutney makes a dream condiment or side to any savoury dish. We like to serve a spoonful on our Super Root Veggie Burgers (see page 68). Using freshly ground cumin seeds brings out more of the flavour of the spice, but you can use ready-ground cumin as an alternative, if easier. The chutney will keep in an airtight container in the refrigerator for up to 1 month.

1 tsp cumin seeds

200g/7oz/1½ cups dried soft pitted dates, roughly chopped

4cm/1½ inch piece of fresh turmeric root, peeled and roughly chopped

2cm/¾ inch piece of fresh root ginger, roughly chopped

100g/3½oz tamarind paste

400ml/14fl oz/1¾ cups water

1 tsp chilli powder

Grind the cumin seeds, if using, in a mini food processor or grinder or using a pestle and mortar. Set aside.

Put the dates, turmeric, ginger and tamarind in a small saucepan and pour in the water. Stir and slowly bring to the boil then turn the heat down and simmer for 5 minutes until the dates start to break down.

Pour the mixture into a food processor and add the chilli powder and ground cumin. Blend to a smooth, thick paste or chutney. Store in the refrigerator for up to 2 weeks.

Treats

Flourless Gingerbread Brownies

Prep and cook: 1 hour,
plus standing
Makes: 12

Linseeds (flaxseeds) make an amazing vegan alternative to eggs. When soaked, they form a jelly-like consistency that works like a binding agent in the same way as eggs do. The seeds are also packed with plant-based omega-3 fats, alpha-linolenic acid and protein, making these a decadent yet healthy gluten-free treat. They will keep in the refrigerator in an airtight container for up to a week.

2 tbsp melted coconut oil, plus extra for greasing

2 tbsp whole linseeds (flaxseeds) or 1½ tbsp ground

100ml/3½fl oz/scant ½ cup water

4 tbsp maple syrup

2 tbsp peanut butter

1 tbsp grated fresh root ginger

1 tsp vanilla extract

100g/3½oz/1 cup raw cacao powder

1 tsp ground cardamom

pinch of salt

Preheat the oven to 180°C/350°F/gas 4. Line the base and grease the sides of a 20cm/8 inch square baking pan with a little coconut oil.

Grind the linseeds in a mini food processor or grinder (it's always best to use freshly ground linseeds as they have a greater nutritional value than ready-ground ones). Tip the linseeds into a mixing bowl, stir in the water and leave to soak for 15 minutes or until they have a jelly-like consistency.

Add the melted coconut oil, maple syrup, peanut butter, grated ginger, vanilla extract and the soaked linseeds and water to the bowl and mix well.

In a separate bowl, mix together the cacao powder, cardamom and salt. Stir the dry ingredients into the wet ingredients until you have a smooth batter.

Pour the mixture into the prepared baking pan and spread out evenly. Bake for 35 minutes until cooked but still slightly gooey. Leave to stand for 30 minutes before turning out and slicing into 12 squares.

Maca Bliss Balls

**Prep: 20 minutes,
plus chilling
Makes: 12**

Coconut butter has a much sweeter and buttery flavour and creamier texture than coconut oil. For best results, ensure that the ingredients are blended well in the food processor. Maca has a beautifully sweet, caramel taste that is rather unique. It is native to the high Andes in Peru but is now readily available in health food stores and supermarkets. It is renowned for its ability to enhance and lift mood, making these decadent bliss balls a heartwarming indulgence.

50g/1¾oz/⅓ cup dried soft pitted dates, roughly chopped

4 tbsp maple syrup

125g/4½oz/½ cup coconut oil, melted

60g/2¼oz/½ cup macadamia nuts

60g/2¼oz/½ cup cashew nuts

2½ tbsp maca powder

4 tbsp coconut butter, such as Coconut Manna

pinch of salt

unsweetened desiccated (shredded) coconut, for coating

Put all the ingredients, except the desiccated coconut, in a food processor and blend thoroughly to make a thick, smooth paste.

Cover a plate with the coconut.

Scoop the date mixture out of the food processor and form into 12 walnut-size balls, then roll each one in the coconut until coated all over.

Chill in the refrigerator for 1 hour to firm up.

Ginger & Cardamom Carrot Pudding

Prep and cook: 1 hour
Serves: 6

A traditional, rich Indian pudding, *gajar ka halwa*, which will send your senses wild. For best results, grind your own cardamom seeds and use freshly grated root ginger. Serve hot, warm or cold with a spoonful of yogurt.

400g/14oz carrots, grated
2 tbsp grated fresh root ginger
400ml/14fl oz/1¾ cups coconut milk
100ml/3½fl oz/scant ½ cup water
handful of raisins
30g/1oz/scant ¼ cup cashew nuts
4 tbsp coconut sugar
3 tbsp melted coconut oil
½ tsp freshly ground green cardamom seeds
thick yogurt and ground cinnamon, to serve (optional)

Put the carrots, ginger and coconut milk in a heavy saucepan. Stir in the water and bring to the boil. Turn the heat down and simmer over a low heat until almost all of the liquid has reduced, stirring frequently with a wooden spoon to ensure it doesn't stick to the base of the pan.

Add the raisins, cashews, coconut sugar, coconut oil and cardamom and continue to cook, stirring frequently, until the liquid has reduced and the mixture has a thick and creamy texture.

Serve in bowls and top with a good spoonful of yogurt and cinnamon, if using.

Turmeric & Coconut Chocolate Truffles

Prep and cook: 45 minutes, plus chilling
Makes: 12

100g/3½oz/1⅓ cups unsweetened desiccated (shredded) coconut

1 tsp vanilla extract

2 tsp Golden Spoon Turmeric Honey (Wunder Workshop or see page 92)

60g/2oz cacao butter

10g/¼oz coconut oil

2 tbsp raw cacao powder, sifted

1 tbsp maple syrup

Chocolate and coconut is one of our favourite flavour combinations and these golden truffle treats are no exception.

To make the filling, put the coconut, vanilla and turmeric honey in a food processor or blender and blend until creamy. The longer you blend the mixture, the creamier the texture will be. Set aside.

For the chocolate coating, put the cacao butter and coconut oil in a bain marie, or heatproof bowl, placed over a pan of simmering water (make sure the bottom doesn't touch the water) and heat gently, stirring, until melted. Remove the bowl from the heat.

Slowly add the cacao powder to the cacao butter mixture, stirring continuously until combined. Add the maple syrup. Leave the cacao mixture to cool to the consistency of treacle.

Pour a little of the cacao mixture into each of the 12 rectangular chocolate moulds – remember the moulds must be deep enough to hold the coconut and turmeric filling. Tilt the moulds so the sides are evenly coated in a layer of chocolate. Leave to set for 10 minutes in the refrigerator.

Spoon the filling mixture into the moulds, then seal the top with a final coating of chocolate. Return to the refrigerator for at least 30 minutes to firm up. Turn the chocolates out of the moulds before serving. They will keep for up to 1 week in the refrigerator.

Golden Almond Butter Cups

Prep and cook: 40 minutes, plus chilling
Makes: 8 petit four-size cups

Almond butter and turmeric add a wonderful twist to the classic chocolate peanut butter cup. Curcumin, one of the active components in turmeric, is not easily absorbed by the body, but combining it with healthy fats, such as coconut oil, encourages absorption.

60g/2oz cacao butter
2 tbsp raw cacao powder
1 tbsp date nectar

Golden filling:
1 tbsp coconut oil
½ tsp turmeric powder
1 tbsp coconut sugar
80g/2¾oz/⅔ cup almond butter

To make the golden filling, melt the coconut oil in a small pan over a low heat. Stir in the turmeric and coconut sugar. Take the pan off the heat, add the almond butter and stir until mixed in. Set aside.

For the chocolate coating, put the cacao butter in a bain marie, or heatproof bowl, placed over a pan of simmering water (make sure the bottom doesn't touch the water) and heat gently, stirring, until melted. Stir in the cacao powder and date nectar until smooth. Leave to cool to the consistency of thick treacle.

Set aside about a quarter of the chocolate to seal the cups and pour 1 tablespoon of the rest of the chocolate into a petit four case. Spread evenly, tilting the cup so the mixture coats the base and sides of the case. Repeat with all eight of the petit four cases. Leave to set in the freezer for 15 minutes.

Once the chocolate has set, spoon the almond butter into the cups until each one is about three-quarters full. Spoon the remaining chocolate over the top of the filling until it is covered, spreading it out to the edge of each cup to seal. Leave to set in the refrigerator for another 15 minutes. The cups will keep in the refrigerator for up to 5 days, if they last that long.

Cocktails

Turmeric Chai-tini

Prep: 10 minutes
Serves: 2

This is a cheeky winter warmer that will spice up any dinner party. It's perhaps easier to prepare a big batch of the turmeric chai before guests arrive and then let it settle – leaving it for longer only enhances the taste and will save you time later. When heating the milk, make sure that it doesn't boil as this will bring out the bitterness of the black tea in the chai. (Pictured opposite, right.)

240ml/8fl oz/1 cup plant-based milk, preferably oat or coconut

2 tsp Wunder Instantly Golden Chai Latte Blend (or homemade blend, see page 38)

2 tbsp vodka

1 tbsp maple syrup or date syrup

ice cubes

cinnamon stick, to serve (optional)

Mix together the plant milk and turmeric chai in a small pan until combined. Heat gently over a low heat for 15 minutes, stirring occasionally and making sure the milk doesn't boil. Leave to cool.

Strain the chai into a cocktail shaker, add the vodka and syrup and top up with ice. Shake vigorously for 20 seconds before straining into martini glasses.

Serve with a cinnamon stick for stirring, if liked.

Fiery Whiskey Sour

Prep: 10 minutes
Serves: 1

The fresh root ginger, a twist on the classic, is like a heart-warming hug. For a vegan option, use aquafaba, which is the protein-rich bean brine found in canned chickpeas (garbanzo beans) and other beans. It is used here as an alternative to the usual egg white. (Pictured page 106, left.)

3 tbsp/2 shots whiskey

1½ tbsp freshly juiced root ginger (about 40g/1½oz piece of fresh root ginger gives this quantity of juice)

2 tbsp aquafaba (the bean brine from a can of chickpeas/garbanzo beans) or 1 egg white

juice of 1 lime

1 tbsp maple syrup

2 dashes Angostura bitters

ice cubes

Put all the ingredients in a cocktail shaker and shake vigorously for 20 seconds.

Add plenty of ice to a rocks glass, strain over the cocktail and serve.

Alternatively, blend all the ingredients in a high-speed blender for a foamy texture before pouring over ice.

[Pictured on page 106, top and left.]

Tropical Golden Rum

Prep: 10 minutes
Serves 1

Pineapple contains an enzyme known as bromelain, which has been shown to increase the bioavailability of turmeric. So what better way to incorporate the golden root than in a tropical pineapple cocktail.

½ pineapple, skin removed and cut into long wedges, plus an extra thin slice to decorate

4cm/1½ inch piece of fresh turmeric root

8cm/3¼ inch piece of fresh root ginger

4cm/1½ inch piece of galangal root

juice and zest of 1 lime

1½ tbsp grapefruit juice

1 tbsp coconut sugar

1½ tbsp/1 shot dark rum

ice cubes

Juice the pineapple, turmeric, ginger and galangal. Add to a cocktail shaker with the lime juice and zest, grapefruit juice and coconut sugar. Top up with ice and shake well.

Pour the rum into a tumbler and add ice. Pour in the contents of the shaker, stir and decorate the glass with a thin slice of pineapple.

Rooty Bitters

**Prep: 5 minutes,
plus 7 days infusing
Makes: 100ml/3½fl oz/
scant ½ cup**

Bitters are fascinating. These concentrated concoctions were traditionally used as medicinal tonics and are made from botanicals such as roots, herbs, fruit or bark, steeped in a neutral-tasting alcohol. Bitters make a great addition to cocktails, creating a complex and deep flavour profile, enhancing and complementing the rest of the ingredients. The process required to extract flavour can take a while and varies depending on the type and quantity of ingredients you are using. Here, we have given you three different flavour options (see overleaf for two more) and the method for creating your own bitters, which can be adapted to create favourite flavour combinations.

Turmeric Bitters

1 tsp grated fresh turmeric root
vodka, for topping up – one with
the least flavour possible

Put the grated turmeric root in a sterilized small mason jar (see page 72), about 100ml/3½fl oz/scant ½ cup in size.

Pour enough vodka into the jar to come about 5mm/¼ inch below the rim. Shut the lid tightly. Label the jar with the flavouring and date and leave for 7 days to infuse. After a week, strain the bitters into a second sterilized jar.

Ginger Bitters

Bitters are incredibly versatile and their use certainly does not have to be restricted to the realm of alcohol. Try adding a few drops of this ginger bitters to liven up sparkling water, desserts or coffee.

1 tsp grated fresh root ginger
vodka, for topping up – one with the least flavour possible

Put the ginger in a sterilized small mason jar (see page 72), about 100ml/3½fl oz/scant ½ cup in size.

Pour enough vodka into the jar to come about 5mm/¼ inch below the rim. Shut the lid tightly. Label the jar with the flavouring and date and leave for 7 days to infuse. After a week, strain the bitters into a second sterilized jar.

Lime Bitters

This fragrant lime-infused bitters, joins the Ginger Bitters (above) and Turmeric Bitters (see page 110) in The ACV cocktail, see opposite.

1 tsp grated lime zest
vodka, for topping up – one with the least flavour possible

Put the lime zest in a sterilized small mason jar (see page 72), about 100ml/3½fl oz/scant ½ cup in size.

Pour enough vodka into the jar to come about 5mm/¼ inch below the rim. Shut the lid tightly. Label the jar with the flavouring and date and leave for 7 days to infuse. After a week, strain the bitters into a second sterilized jar.

The ACV

Prep: 5 minutes
Serves: 1

1 tsp Turmeric Bitters
(see page 110)

1 tsp Ginger Bitters (see opposite)

1 tsp Lime Bitters (see opposite)

1½ tbsp/1 shot gin

1 tsp runny honey

1 tbsp raw, unfiltered apple
cider vinegar

150ml/5fl oz/scant ⅔ cup
sparkling water

ice cubes

sprig of rosemary

We love making cocktails and experimenting with all kinds of super roots and other healthy ingredients. Interestingly, alcohol synergizes with turmeric and is said to increase the bioavailability of the root.

Shake all the ingredients, apart from the rosemary and ice cubes, in a cocktail shaker.

Pour into a tumbler over ice and use the sprig of rosemary to stir.

Apothecary

Golden Facemask

Prep: 5 minutes
Makes: 1

In Sri Lanka, a full body wrap made with turmeric paste is a popular Ayurvedic treatment for calming insect bites. Turmeric's powerful anti-inflammatory and anti-bacterial properties are also good for treating acne and blemishes. Be warned though, turmeric can stain everything it comes into contact with, so be careful with towels and clothes. Also, wash your face well afterwards to avoid staining. It is best to remove the mask just before you shower so that you can thoroughly remove it.

1 tbsp chickpea (gram) flour
1 tsp turmeric powder
2 tbsp rosewater

Mix together all the ingredients into a paste. Apply the mask evenly all over your cleansed face and leave on for 10–15 minutes.

Wash off the mask with lukewarm water, then have a shower to remove it thoroughly. Dry your face gently with a clean towel.

Joint Wrap

Prep: 5 minutes
Makes: 1

Joint pain can be due to excessive exercise or chronic conditions such as arthritis. Alongside your usual medication or treatment, the following wrap can assist in relieving symptoms and reducing swelling. Coconut oil, ginger and frankincense are natural anti-inflammatories and when applied directly to the painful area can permeate the skin with a soothing effect.

6 drops ginger essential oil
3 drops frankincense essential oil
3 tbsp coconut oil

Mix together the ginger, frankincense and coconut oil to make a paste.

Apply and gently massage the paste into the painful joint area and leave for 10–15 minutes – use a dressing to hold the mixture in place if necessary.

When ready, use warm water to remove the oil mixture and pat the area dry.

Glowing Ashwagandha Toner

Prep: 5 minutes
Makes: 1

The antioxidant ashwagandha is said to stimulate the production of natural oils in the skin, helping to keep it hydrated. It contains active ingredients known as withanolides that can rid the skin of impurities, and due to their anti-inflammatory qualities can reduce redness. The high levels of vitamin C in the lemon helps to naturally boost collagen production and the citrus fruit is also anti-bacterial.

½ tsp ashwagandha root powder
½ tsp ground ginger
juice of 1 lemon

Mix together all the ingredients to make a paste.

Apply the mask evenly all over your cleansed face and leave it on for 10 minutes.

Wash off the mask with lukewarm water, then dry your face gently with a cloth and apply moisturizer.

Ayurvedic Anti-anxiety Bath Soak

Prep: 10 minutes
Makes: 1

In Ayurvedic medicine, a warm ginger bath is recommended to treat anxiety. The ginger is said to activate the parasympathetic nervous system (PNS), the rest system that helps to slow the heart rate and relax muscles. It also increases circulation and therefore can help to soothe muscles or joint soreness.

60g/2¼oz finely grated fresh root ginger

60g/2¼oz/¼ cup bicarbonate of soda (baking soda)

80g/2¾oz/¾ cup Epsom salts

5 drops sandalwood essential oil (or other calming PNS-activating essential oil such as lavender, orange or rosemary)

Mix all the ingredients together to make a coarse paste. Add the paste to your bath tub and fill with warm water – swish the water around to evenly distribute the bath soak.

Take a restful bath for 15 minutes, breathing deeply to unwind and let go.

Burdock Tea & Toner

Prep and cook: 25 minutes, plus cooling
Serves: 1

This recipe makes a simple tea-cum-skin toner, and is inspired by Korean beauty regimes that treat acne-prone skin both from the inside and out. Internally, the tea helps to cleanse the body of toxins, while topically it neutralizes the toxins that can cause skin problems. It is an anti-inflammatory and helps to heal blemishes.

2 tbsp dried burdock root pieces
480ml/16fl oz/2 cups water

Place the burdock root and water in a saucepan and bring to the boil. Turn the heat down and simmer for 20 minutes.

Turn off the heat and strain the liquid into a jug. Pour half into a mug and drink as a tea while still warm. (Burdock root contains, inulin, among other nutrients. This prebiotic fibre is good for gut flora, and the health of the gut affects the health of the skin.)

Pour the remaining tea into a sterilized jar (see page 72) and leave to cool. Once cool, use as a skin toner (or it can be used as a cleanser). Using cotton wool, pat it onto the skin after cleansing and before moisturizing.

Store in the refrigerator for up to 4 days.

Dandelion Root Steam

Homemade facial steam baths are a great way to get rid of congestion and tonify the skin. The steam from the dandelion- and calendula-infused water can help to open up pores, soften blackheads and get rid of dead skin cells and any impurities.

10g/½oz dried calendula flower petals

2 tbsp dandelion root (or dandelion root tea bags)

1 litre/35fl oz/4¼ cups water

Place the calendula and dandelion in a pan with the water and bring to the boil. Turn the heat down and let it simmer for 5 minutes to infuse.

Leave to cool slightly and carefully pour everything into a bowl.

Hold your cleansed face above the steaming water, making sure it has cooled down enough so you don't scorch it, for 15 minutes. Place a towel over your head to maximize the steam. Finish by patting your face dry.

Roots Directory

There are plenty of health food stores and supermarkets that stock the more common root spices such as turmeric, ginger, galangal, maca, nettle root and liquorice, but some of the less familiar roots mentioned in this book may be more difficult to find. We therefore recommend the following online retailers:

G Baldwin & Co
www.baldwins.co.uk

Indigo Herbs®
www.indigo-herbs.co.uk

Planet Organic
www.planetorganic.com

Buy Wholedfoods Online
www.buywholefoodsonline.co.uk

iHerb®
www.iherb.com

Amazon
www.amazon.co.uk
www.amazon.com

Just Ingredients
www.justingredients.co.uk

Index

Thank You

We would like to give a special mention to Valeria Huerta, whose support made all of this happen. To the wonderful team at Pavilion, in particular, Stephanie Milner whose enthusiasm has driven this book from start to finish. Nicola Graimes, Laura Russell, Emily Breen, Sarah Epton and Laura Brodie for their patient dedication and attention to detail. Also, to Kitty Coles, Madeleine Montau-Andrews, Dan Jones and Linda Berlin whose talents have made everything so beautiful.

Tom would like to dedicate this book to his family for their never-ending support and to his friends for their enduring interest in turmeric.

Zoë would like to dedicate this work to her late mother for her continuing guidance and inspiration; her family and friends for believing in her and for always being open to trying our weird and wonderful creations.